And Still the Turtle Watched

And still the

Turtle Watched

by Sheila MacGill-Callahan

pictures by Barry Moser

PUFFIN BOOKS

PUFFIN BOOKS
Published by the Penguin Group
Penguin Putnam Books for Young Readers, 345 Hudson Street, New York, New York 10014, U.S.A.
Penguin Books Ltd, 80 Strand, London WC2R ORL, England
Penguin Books Australia Ltd, Ringwood, Victoria, Australia
Penguin Books Canada Ltd, 10 Alcorn Avenue, Toronto, Ontario, Canada M4V 3B2
Penguin Books (N.Z.) Ltd, 182-190 Wairau Road, Auckland 10, New Zealand
Penguin Books Ltd, Registered Offices: Harmondsworth, Middlesex, England

First published by Dial Books for Young Readers,
a division of Penguin Books USA Inc., 1991
First published by Puffin Books, 1996

20 19 18 17 16 15 14 13 12

Designed by Barry Moser
Calligraphy by Reassurance Wunder

THE LIBRARY OF CONGRESS HAS CATALOGED THE DIAL EDITION AS FOLLOWS:
MacGill-Callahan, Sheila.
And still the turtle watched/Sheila MacGill-Callahan;
pictures by Barry Moser.—1st ed.
p. cm.
Summary: A turtle carved in rock on a bluff over a river by Indians long ago,
watches with sadness the changes man brings over the years.
ISBN 0-8037-0931-5.—ISBN 0-8037-0932-3 (lib.bdg.)
[1. Turtles—Fiction. 2. Man—Influence on nature—Fiction.]
I. Moser, Barry, ill. II. Title.
PZ7.M16765An 1991 [Fic]—dc20 90-37377 CIP AC

Puffin Books ISBN 0-14-055836-5
Manufactured in China

*The illustrations were painted with transparent watercolor on paper handmade for the Royal Watercolor Society
by Simon Green. They were then color-separated and reproduced as red, blue, yellow, and black halftones.*

For Leo—S.M-C.

For Jane, for good friendship and good counsel
—B.M.

LONG AGO when the eagles still built their nests on the cliffs by the river, an old man and his grandson stood beside a large rock.

The rock stood all by itself on the bluff at the bend in the river where the bright water flowed to the bitter sea.

"Here at our summer lodge," the old man said, "I will carve the turtle. He will be the eyes of Manitou the All-Father to watch the Delaware people and he will be our voice to speak to Manitou. In summer you will bring your children to the rock to greet the turtle and they will bring their children. And Manitou will bless our land with plenty, our people with straight bodies and strong arms, and peace shall reign beside our fires."

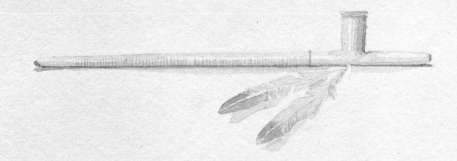

And so he shaped the stone. And then the turtle
watched.

He watched the green of summer turn to the gold of autumn.

He watched the gold of autumn become the white of winter.

He watched the white of winter give birth to the flowers of springtime.

Then summer came again. The turtle was happiest in summer, for then the children came. And then their children, and then their children's children's children.

Year followed year. The Great Bear chased the Little Bear around and around the northern sky. As time wore on, fewer and fewer children came to greet the turtle. Have I watched badly? he thought. Does Manitou no longer hear me?

The rains washed him, the winds blew him, countless snows chilled him, blowing dust rubbed him. Now it took a sharp and knowing eye to see the turtle.

Then one day strangers came. They did not greet the turtle. They did not speak to Manitou. Their axes chopped and killed the forest. Their shouting drowned the lark's bright music. The turtle watched, but did not understand.

He watched as stranger followed stranger followed stranger.

He watched white water turn to brown. He felt the air grow heavy. He heard strange growling noises still the song of birds.

At night new lights glowed near the ground. They dimmed the stars of Manitou.

The little turtle grew very sad. Why do I watch? he thought. Why do I speak to Manitou when Manitou no longer hears me? The air is dark and dirty. The stars are dim. The noises hurt my ears. My children have not come for many times many moons.

In the night the turtle wept.

One day some boys came near the rock. They stopped and pointed. The turtle's heart beat faster. "They've come to see me," he murmured to himself. "My children have returned. Thank you, Manitou."

He watched them as they capered around him. Black boxes on their shoulders blared loud noise that hurt the turtle's ears. They pointed shiny round things at him.

The turtle heard a hiss. He saw a shining arc of color leap toward him. He felt cool wetness on his eyes. He could no longer see. He could no longer watch for Manitou. Deep in his darkness he felt the cracking of his heart.

No one watched for Manitou as days, months, and years passed, and the turtle stood in darkness. Then one day a man came. He knew that the Delaware people had once summered here. He hoped to find something they had left behind, but searched all day and found nothing. He was tired. He was going home.

Suddenly he saw the rock standing all by itself on the bluff at the bend in the river where the bright water flows to the bitter sea.

Something about the rock called to him as it stood forlorn and covered with graffiti. He was a man who saw beneath what first appeared. He had a sharp and knowing eye, he had a wise and loving heart, he knew the ways of Manitou.

The turtle did not know the man was there. The paint had blinded his eyes. The paint had stopped up his ears. Then he felt a finger on his head. It stroked back along his carapace and he shivered deep inside.

The man came back with workmen. They pried the rock out of the ground and hoisted it up on a truck. The little turtle was very frightened. He did not know what was happening.

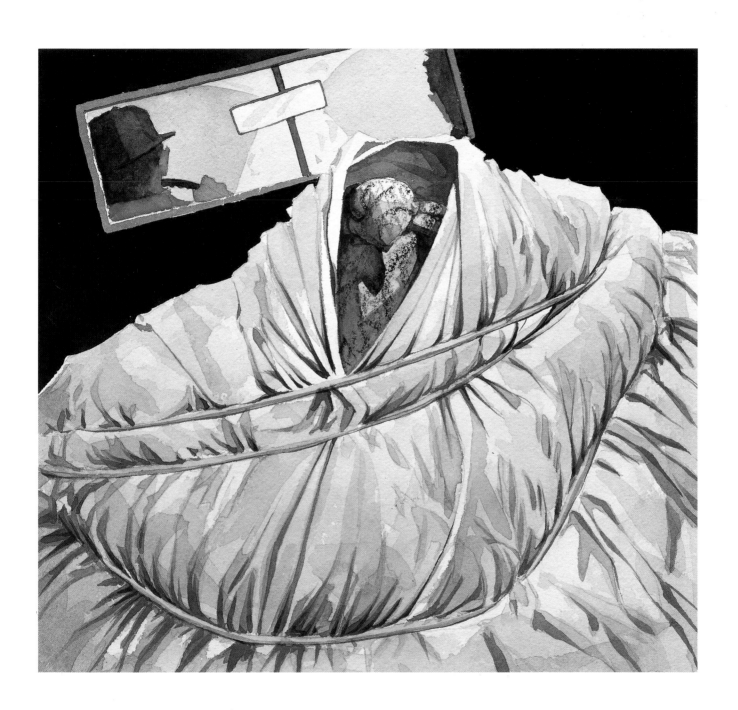

The truck swayed and bumped along for a long long time. Then the rock was hoisted off the truck. Hands patted and rubbed the turtle. He felt sharp-smelling wetness pour over his head and his eyes started to clear and his ears to hear as the paint was scrubbed away.

No longer is he watching by the river. He is indoors at the botanical garden where the children come to see him. And they will bring their children, and their children's children's children. And he will speak of them to Manitou.

If you live in or visit New York City you can see the turtle at the Watson Building of the New York Botanical Garden. Weathered and worn, its features are no longer so distinct, although its basic shape and nature can still be seen by those who know and believe.